Chaotic Harmony

A TMA Student Anthology Project

Chaotic Harmony

A TMA Student Anthology Project

Edited by Dr. Rhonda M. Lawson,
Meet the World Image Solutions

Co-edited by TJ Hendrix,
TMA Anthology Project Coordinator

Chaotic Harmony

Edited by
Dr. Rhonda M. Lawson

Published by Meet the World Image Solutions

P.O. Box 8803
New Orleans, LA 70182
www.mtwimagesolutions.com
Copyright © 2022

For permissions, contact:
info@mtwimagesolutions.com

Cover design by Thurgood Marshall Academy Students

Thurgood Marshall Academy
Public Charter High School
2427 Martin Luther King, Jr. Avenue, SE,
Washington, DC 20020
Malika Mays, Head of School

ISBN: 979-8-9872429-0-2
Meet the World Image Solutions

Dedication

In depth of gratitude, we dedicate this book to the unheard,
the unseen, the tired, and the restless.

To the Warriors we lost and the Warriors who are lost,
this book is for you.

Table of Contents

Foreword

Writing.

I find writing to be the most difficult medium to share information, thoughts, or just curiosities. Writing demands a level of energy and precision that, when done well, is relevant and long-lasting. Writing pulls thoughts from one's mind and places them securely on paper, or rather the screen here in the 21st century. The writer hopes others "get it."

Writing makes authors question their intent, outcomes, and placement of words, phrases, and punctuation to be sure the message is not conflated. Writing, as my 8th-grade teacher would probably say, is what moves our community to be greater tomorrow than we are today.

Chaotic Harmony is a collection from a few of the hundreds of brilliant young leaders at Thurgood Marshall Academy. The poems, short stories, opinions and art are from their hearts. Their courage to share with us is a gift. Their words prove that our community will move one step closer to being greater than we ever imagined.

We know you will enjoy their efforts.

Raymond Weeden
Thurgood Marshall Academy
Executive Director

Chaotic Thoughts

Essays and Short Stories

Be The Person You Needed Growing Up

By Mikayla Lewis

Growing up, I was the only girly-girl. For everything, from makeup, to boys, to how to dress girly, I had to learn on my own.

And being deaf and guided by silence, it's really hard to hear if you're doing things right.

I don't know sign language or how to read lips. I asked yes or no questions, but that only misguided me more because there were complications in those lessons. I had to learn from those perfect pretty white girls on YouTube and Google Images (because that's always what we click on to search for something). Their way of doing things never worked for me.

In a way, I'm the person I needed growing up, and I hope I can be that guidance for my sister. I hope she knows no matter how mad I am at her, she can still come to me, and I will guide her down the path that's best for her.

Even though I never had guidance, I can still provide it because my adolescence guided me through everything.

Emari by Safiya Gaskins

The Broken School System

By Henry Walker

My Name is Henry Walker, and I am 17 years old. I live in Washington D.C., and I am a 12th Grader at Thurgood Marshall Academy.

I have noticed the school system has not been doing its job for a while. I'm here to express the issue with schools and how they teach kids to perceive society.

I believe the school system has four levels: the Board of Education, the school's administration, teachers, and the students.

Let's start with why the school system doesn't work. It all goes back to why schools were created in the first place. They were created during the industrial age to produce factory workers. Workers had to follow directions from their managers and do as they were told. Schools are nearly identical in this way.

Think of a prison. The people who are detained have no say in what goes on in this place where they have to stay for multiple hours of their lives. In a way, schools are the same. That's the way society produced people in the 20th century.

In the 21st century, society relies more on the people who can work together and produce their own ideas, and then build off of the ideas of another person. When students come to class, they must do as they are told. Those who follow the directions get labeled as perfect students who will succeed in life. Transversely, those who don't get called academically challenged and are told they'll be flipping burgers at McDonald's.

Schools were created to prepare people for the world. The world is different and has evolved dramatically since the late 1800s and 1900s, yet school has remained the same for over a century. The 20th-century learners and 21st-century learners are uniquely different. While 20th-century learners see the world as black and white (metaphorically), 21st-century learners can see the different colors in the world.

The world doesn't need more factory workers; it needs innovative thinkers.

Each level in the school system plays a part in why schools fail students. The Federal Department of Education is at the top nationally. They distribute funds to counties, towns, and even states. Nationally, the Department of Education writes the standards and tells schools what and how they should teach. They use outdated methods even though society has the technology and tools to properly prepare students for the world.

Representatives on the local level distribute finances unfairly. The schools' administrations are just as much to blame as the Federal Department of Education. They treat kids like robots, and not people.

Teachers, administrators, and the school board claim they are all about our education. My question is how can you take kids away from their education because of something like a bonnet or a hoodie? Schools are more worried about kids following rules than understanding their work.

The Federal Department of Education is really at fault. They're the ones who give more resources to schools with better test scores. Children from those schools tend to show better academic success, while students from the schools that don't receive adequate resources are left to struggle academically.

Now, if the roles were reversed, I strongly believe administrators as a whole would see a drastic change from an academic standpoint of the kids who receive, and those who don't receive the resources needed to succeed.

To help these students, we need to first give them equal funding. Treat all kids just as they are—the future of this world.

To make school better, we must look at the problem. Modern employment values aren't upheld in schools today. Jobs value creativity, critical thinking skills, cooperation with others, and rational thinking. Without these skills being taught at the high school level, kids will graduate with a diploma knowing the area of a square or what happened in 1941, but they won't be prepared for a job that asks their opinion or asks them to solve a real-world problem.

I think we should start with the 11th and 12th grade students all over the nation by giving them the choice of what class they want to take. We need real classes like agriculture (how to grow and sell crops), robotics class (for engineers), and classes that teach how to invest, build, get a job, etc. These classes will better support learners by giving them some type of experience.

A Familiar Scene: 1968

By Rahkeam Pickens

Some argue that the only answer to a riot is a bullet, while others cry that progress comes from uprising in the streets.

In the months and years leading up to the 1968 election, anti-war protests grew frequent across the country with larger crowds turning out. This resulted in some states increasing their response to the protestors, which quickly turned into confrontations. It wasn't just anti-war protests, but tired minority groups as well.

Flashing back to the summer of 1966, Chicago's Westside was engulfed in flames, shell casings and shattered storefronts. The scene was the same across millions of television sets across the nation. Conservatives and the Republican party took the opportunity to paint the left as a party of lawlessness, and their efforts only grew stronger as dozens of cities were besieged by violent riots in 1968, spanning from Chicago, Baltimore, Detroit, New York City, and the Nation's Capital in the wake of the slayings of Rev. Martin Luther King, Jr., and presidential candidate Robert Kennedy.

A tired Black population had grown restless to unkept promises while in the South, and some white populations began to resist federal integration. A long-brewing storm engulfed cities across the nation. The storm reached its peak in August of 1968 when presidential candidate Hubert Humphrey visited Chicago while on the campaign trail. Humphrey had long been a supporter of nonviolence, but now, the violence was at his doorstep.

As riot police and the National Guard mobilized in Chicago and surrounded protesters and rioters alike, the Democratic National Convention was taking place. Unlike previous conventions, this one took place behind barbed wire, blockades and National Guardsmen with orders to shoot to kill if necessary.

With the National Guard deployed in over a dozen cities across the country, including the Nation's Capital, it seemed as though the country was on the verge of a second Civil War, almost similar to the Summer of 2020 in the wake of George Floyd's murder in Minneapolis, Minnesota, which also took place during an election year.

2022 Civil Rights Trip Reflection

By Rahkeam Pickens

The Civil Rights Trip is a school-sponsored trip for students to learn about the Civil Rights Movement where it took place. For the past five years or so, TMA has taken dozens of students to Alabama, Mississippi, Georgia, and Tennessee. Students learn new aspects of the Civil Rights Movement, speak to survivors and crusaders, touch pieces of history, and—the most touching part—walk the Edmund Pettus Bridge. Students are left with memories and emotions that a textbook or video cannot evoke, and I hope every student turns those emotions into motivation for activism.

The 2022 Spring Break Civil Rights Trip didn't just give me a better understanding of the movement; it introduced me to an entirely new perspective. For so long, every time we've been taught about Civil Rights, it's always taught as though it was a movement of the past, an ancient relic of some kind.

Like others, I, too, held that thought, but that notion was proven untrue with the Summer of 2020. The Black Lives Matter (BLM) Movement is a social justice group that was founded in 2013 and took off in the wake of George Floyd's death in Minneapolis in the summer of 2020.

I had so many questions. I felt misled. Every media outlet on every channel and social media page had images of violent riots, vandalizers and looters. I didn't know what to believe.

I had the movement in my backyard; they were in Washington! So, I took to doing some exploring on my own. For a while, my questions went unanswered.

How do you fight the system and win?

All cops can't be bad, can they?

I sat down and talked to older people who were alive during the Civil Rights Movement, some of whom even marched.

In Tennessee, we saw the lighter side of the dark truth—African-American movers and shakers in the 20th century who got their start on Beale Street. We stood outside the "I Am A Man" memorial. I walked the timeline of the protest. To retrace those steps event for event almost put us in the moment.

Our walking tour was turned into a sightseeing bus tour due to the rain and logistics of moving eighty students, but I preferred the bus tour, anyway. Our lively tour guide drove us past W.C. Handy's shotgun home, which is quite literally just a one-room shack. She showed us the church where Ida B. Wells challenged white supremacy and segregationists from the basement.

In Mississippi, we visited Tougaloo College, which sat on the most beautiful grounds with old southern oaks that reminded me of a scene from *Gone with the Wind*, a complicated film in itself. In a way, that reminder was accurate. Tougaloo sits on the land of a former slave plantation. In fact, the master's house still sits on the property, just steps away from one of the finest HBCUs. We walked on ground that we would have *worked* on some 150 years ago. One day, some of us will be walking those grounds as college graduates. Imagine trying to explain *that* to a slave master!

We saw what remains of the grocery store where Emmet Till was accused of flirting with a white girl. That's the very place where his fate was decided. Not even a week later, Till, who was only 14, was taken from his uncle's home. I don't think *killed* exposes light on the truth enough here. Instead, I prefer to use *executed* because that's just what they did to him—they took the life of a child.

The courthouse where the trial took place had polished wooden floors and long dark benches. The natural light almost made me forget that one of the greatest injustices took place in that courtroom. A betrayal of the American legal system.

We know for a fact the legal system is broken today, but I couldn't begin to imagine trying to find justice in a system that refuses to acknowledge your humanity. Sitting in the courtroom where Mamie Till was denied justice was a revelation moment for me. Imagine all those crushed Black voices whose stories we don't hear.

The trip took history from a textbook and put it in your face. The good, the bad, and the half of humanity I wish didn't exist. The trip answered all of my questions about the Civil Rights Movement.

Five years from now, I hope every student has the opportunity to take such a trip. To see history where it happened, to know there are personalities to these figures we hear so much about, or to meet the people who dined with, lived with, or simply met these figures is enough to put tears into your eyes. The pain of the movement is very much alive and reminds you that time may pass, but the story is still the same and we all have so much more to learn.

Looking back at the Summer of 2020 and the murder of George Floyd, it reminded me that it happened only five days after my birthday. A week of celebration was halted. What was supposed to be a summer of relaxation was turned into a nightmare as I hoped my friends and family who marched would come back safely.

When people take to the streets, it's the cry of the unheard, the restless, the tired of being tired. I vividly recall going to Capitol Hill in what I call *quiet periods* between the protests. The boarded-up windows had the most beautiful art on them and the scaffolding of buildings were covered with demands for social justice and the names of slain Black men and women. That was the summer I realized I was tired of being just a student; I wanted to be an activist. I'll forever be grateful for the Civil Rights Trip for reinforcing that idea in me.

In the words of my late grandmother, "If you don't use it, lose it." With everything at the touch of a button, I now have everything I need, so I'm going to use it. Use every tool at your disposal to be heard when your voice alone is not enough.

Fight the system with your voices, not violence. Fight for the rights of not just your kind, but every creed or color that's oppressed or disadvantaged.

Photos by
Rahkeam Pickens

14

HARRIET

By Mikayla Lewis

I have a friend who calls me *HARRIET*.

At first, I thought it was racist because of how dark I am, but now I love that nickname. Why? Because...

HARRIET led our people to freedom
- *So,* the chains and whips won't pierce our skin anymore.
- *So,* we can be free to pray to the Lord.
- *So,* we can see our families again.
- *So,* we can be *FREE!*
- *So,* we can be FREE!
- *So,* we can be...*what*?

We aren't free. I'm still seeing my Black brothers and sisters getting beaten, bodies laid out on the street. I see what some of those crackers don't see. I see hope so we can all be free.

We all want the same thing, but think differently. That's why we fight and create all this violence. Instead of coming together, those crackers team up in silence. They stormed the Capitol and there was only one dead body, but if it were our people or people of color, there would be another day off of work or school to mourn the deaths of our Black people. But instead of mourning, we'll just forget. Instead of mourning, we'll do something else—like pay rent.

So, while some are wading in the water or swinging low in their sweet chariots waiting for God to come carry them home, those crackers are trying to shatter our skin like glass because they're trying to figure out if our Black cracks. Well, I can tell you right now: it *don't*, and it *won't*. Our Black will never crack!

Our melanin is something you wish you had, something you wish you could harvest. You steal EVERYTHING from us, yet y'all still not happy! You hate us. I know you do! You want us dead so the world only sees people like you.

So, to FREEDOM I go, and to FREEDOM I'll carry my people because I have a friend who calls me
HARRIET.

Adrianna
Pittman
5/6/22

Ainia and Jojo by Adrianna Pittman

Ainia and Jojo: One to Ten

By Adrianna Pittman

Phone 1:

> **Pick between numbers 1 to 10**
> Ainia

> I pick 2
> JoJo

> **Who do you consider your best friend?**
> Ainia

> You already know who
> JoJo

> **Jojo, just answer 🍔**
> Ainia

> You.
> JoJo

> **I never would have guessed 😊**
> Ainia

> Shut up.
> JoJo

Phone 2:

> **1 to 10, minus 2**
> Ainia

> 1
> JoJo

> **Who would you consider telling all your dirty little secrets?**
> Ainia

> Not you.
> JoJo

> **Ouch. Then who?**
> Ainia

> Paris
> JoJo

> **Why him? Doesn't he hate you with a burning passion?**
> Ainia

> He's my brother
> JoJo

...Fair enough. 3 to 10.
Ainia

3
JoJo

Jesus, pick random numbers and stop trying to go in order!
Ainia

Just ask the question
JoJo

Fine, who are you interested in?
Ainia

Not saying
JoJo

You gotta answer.
Ainia

No, I don't
JoJo

You signed up for this game so you gotta play by the rules
Ainia

I can leave
JoJo

Wait, please don't. I'll be lonely. 🙁
Ainia

We have school tomorrow
JoJo

So?
Ainia

We'll see each other
JoJo

I forgot. But we hardly have any classes together.
Ainia

Math, ELA and Spanish
JoJo

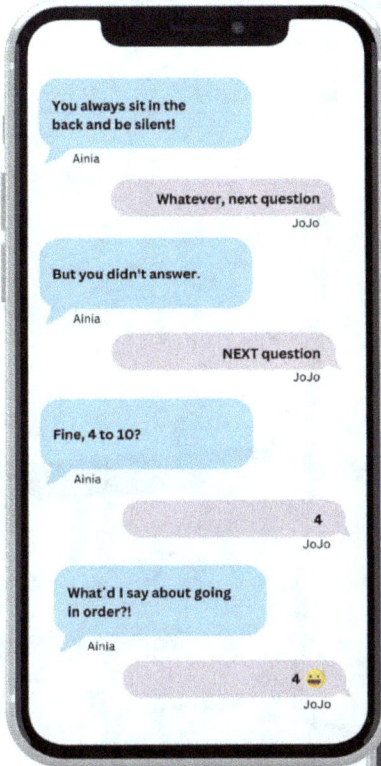

Who do you trust with your life?

Ainia

You

JoJo

...pardon?

Ainia

Read the text over 😊

JoJo

I know but, me? Don't get me wrong, I'm glad but why?

Ainia

You're my friend

JoJo

Wow. That was corny. 😃

Ainia

Next question

JoJo

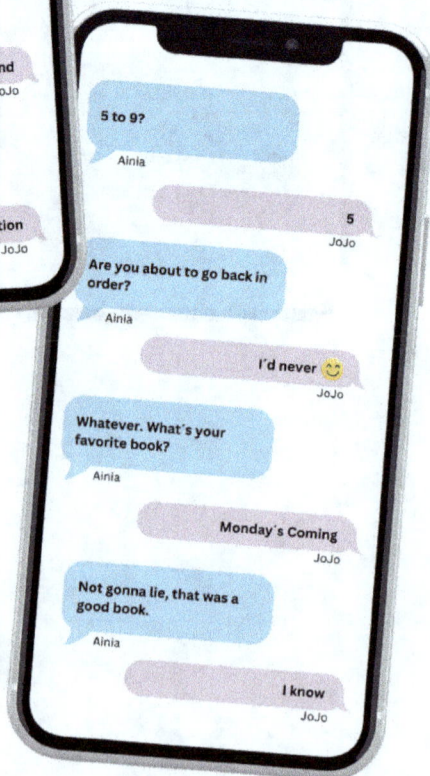

5 to 9?

Ainia

5

JoJo

Are you about to go back in order?

Ainia

I'd never 😊

JoJo

Whatever. What's your favorite book?

Ainia

Monday's Coming

JoJo

Not gonna lie, that was a good book.

Ainia

I know

JoJo

It was also based off a real life event
Ainia

I´m aware
JoJo

6 to 9
Ainia

9
JoJo

How´re all your grades?
Ainia

All A´s
JoJo

Figures. 6 to 8
Ainia

No more commentary?
JoJo

What is there to say? It was to be expected.
Ainia

Then why ask?
JoJo

These were all questions I prepared beforehand! 🙁
Ainia

Whatever. 6
JoJo

What's your favorite subject?
Ainia

Spanish
JoJo

Really?
Ainia

Really
JoJo

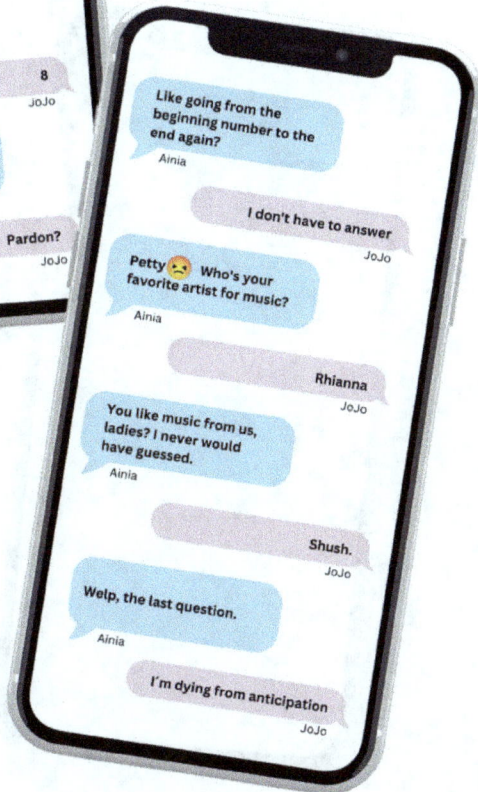

Shush, 10 to 20?

Ainia

10

JoJo

Who do you trust with your life?

Ainia

You.

JoJo

Aww, the same cheesy answer. How adorable

Ainia

I will choke you.

JoJo

I'd like to see you try, I am still stronger than you

Ainia

Maybe, but I'm smarter

JoJo

JOJO LEFT THE CHAT

...Night.

Ainia

AINIA LEFT THE CHAT

Deepest Unknown Emotion

By Nevaeh Fleming

I want to symbolize the feelings Telemachus felt. I want to talk about how the book brings attention to words and how big an impact they can make on the meaning a single word can hold.

Through my poems, I want to write about different emotions and capture the rawest version of what I think he felt. In the book *The Odyssey*, I want to show the feelings Telemachus could have felt throughout the lines he expressed. In my art and poetry, you can determine for yourself what he could be feeling from the point of view of a son who lost his father, and the father trying to get back to his family.

Telemachus goes through so much during his time looking for his father, and even the life before he searched for his father. In *The Odyssey*, you can tell he has these feelings that are being thrown around because of how pent up they are. For example, Telemachus says, "But now, look, you load my heart with grief. There's nothing I can do."

This example relates to the real world throughout the book by expressing emotions of helplessness and sadness that even Telemachus has experienced.

The Odyssey also says "filled with anger, down on the ground he dashed the speaker's scepter bursting into tears. All just sat there silent." This anger is also what real-world people deal. Anger is associated with negativity, and a lot is going around in the world. *The Odyssey* points out his frustration with the situation at home involving his mother and many men looking to use her. *The Odyssey* also says, "So high and mighty, Telemachus-such unbridled rage."

This expresses more and more in-depth emotions.

Telemachus also holds a lot of anger inside of him. I feel Telemachus has a valid reason to be angry. If you have read the book, you would think so, too. I feel the suitors were terrible men. I'll bet the mother wasn't giving up anything, and the men only used her.

I want to convey through the three poems I have written that emotions can be turned into an unspeakable language. Feelings or emotions can be represented in infinite ways. My poetry will relay the idea of many options, to feel feelings and express them as you wish. The reader can try to relate through the poems to Telemachus without even reading the book.

The three poems are titled *Language in Which We Say* Parts 1, 2 and 3. My hope is you can find a new way to express yourself. I also hope you are open to any idea of expressing feelings and finding the way you express feelings currently within yourself. When you do this deep self evaluation, you will start to better understand yourself and your feelings, and how to express those feelings even if it's not through words. Maybe with my help, you can start.

Another quote from *The Odyssey* that dealt with the show of emotions was "and the way you loosened the dogs of this boy's anger...incite this boy to riot." This quote was in the part of the book where other people talked about his lost father. They said cruel things that set off Telemachus, who was often mad and angry about their words.

Even if you don't read the book, you can tell by the quote that he is terribly mad. To describe his anger as loose dogs who presumably are wild and loud and rambunctious is to describe Telemachus's feelings. He is so angry that some call it a riot.

Another sign of emotion from Telemachus was seen in this quote in the scene before Telemachus meets his father: "Telemachus, no more shyness, this is not the time...someone my age might feel shy."

Telemachus goes on to say, "someone my age might feel shy."

In this quote, he shares his feelings through words, but the act of feeling shy might show in different ways, such as facial expression, tone, and etc.

A quote from class says, "Boys are taught to not let out their emotions even though it's perfectly okay to show emotions...But I understand society's ideals getting in the way and blocking...sad thoughts."

This describes Telemachus meeting his father and the reaction to the emotions he displayed "before he had always reigned his emotions back."

This show of emotion was real and raw. In class, I said, "I think he cried because sometimes words trigger deep unknown emotion, whether you wanted to hear it or not. It could be something you tried to block out that found a way to rise up in your mind."

Language is not always words. Words cannot always portray the feelings that you are truly feeling. I hope you can relate to the emotional expressions that can be language or something above that. Try to better understand yourself for yourself and live to be happy with that outcome. I want everyone to find that deepest unknown emotion and accept its wonder.

Ainia, Jojo, and Friend by Adrianna Pittman

Ainia and Jojo: Ten to Twenty

By Adrianna Pittman

Ainia: Hi, Jojo

JoJo: What now?

Ainia: Pick between 10 and 20

JoJo: We played this yesterday

Ainia: Sure, but that was 1 to 10. This is 10 to 20.

JoJo: 10th question the same?

Ainia: Well, duh, what'd you expect?

JoJo: Better.

Ainia: Shush, 10 to 20?

JoJo: 10

Ainia: Who do you trust with your life?

JoJo: You.

Ainia: Aww, the same cheesy answer. How adorable

JoJo: I will choke you.

Ainia: I'd like to see you try, I am still stronger than you

JoJo: Maybe, but I'm smarter

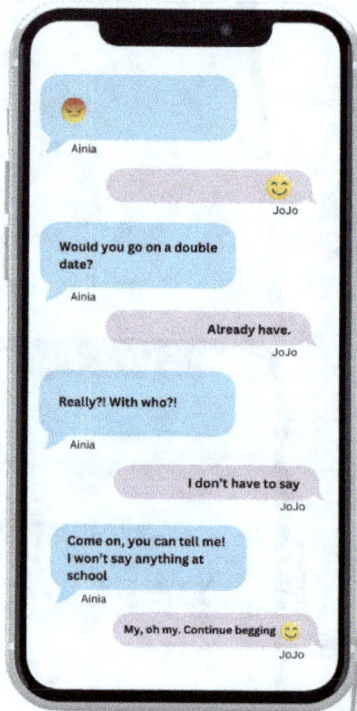

How am I actually the immature one when you indulge in it?????

Ainia

Next question.

JoJo

Oh, got nothing witty to say about that, huh? 😊

Ainia

I just need you to hurry.

JoJo

Whatever Whatever. 12 to 18?

Ainia

13

JoJo

13? I was expecting 12.

Ainia

Ainia.

JoJo

Fine, what's your all time favorite memory?

Ainia

I can't say.

JoJo

What do you mean? You can't remember or somethin'?

Ainia

No, there's hardly any.

JoJo

Then focus on the few you have. Duh.

Ainia

I don't know.

JoJo

Whhaa!?!?!?! You don't have any favorite times with me????

Ainia

I'm not saying that.

JoJo

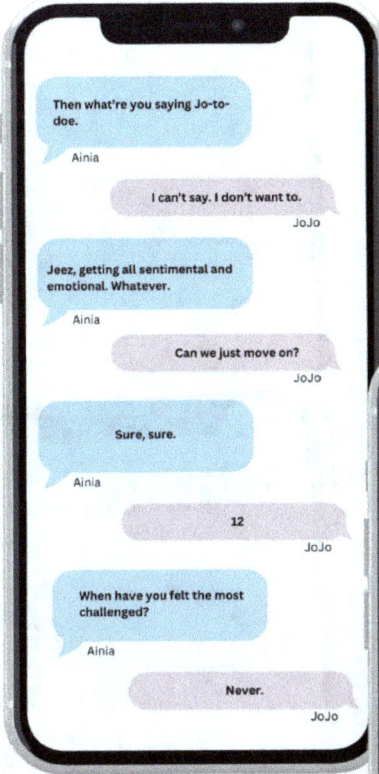

Then what're you saying Jo-to-doe.

Ainia

I can't say. I don't want to.

JoJo

Jeez, getting all sentimental and emotional. Whatever.

Ainia

Can we just move on?

JoJo

Sure, sure.

Ainia

12

JoJo

When have you felt the most challenged?

Ainia

Never.

JoJo

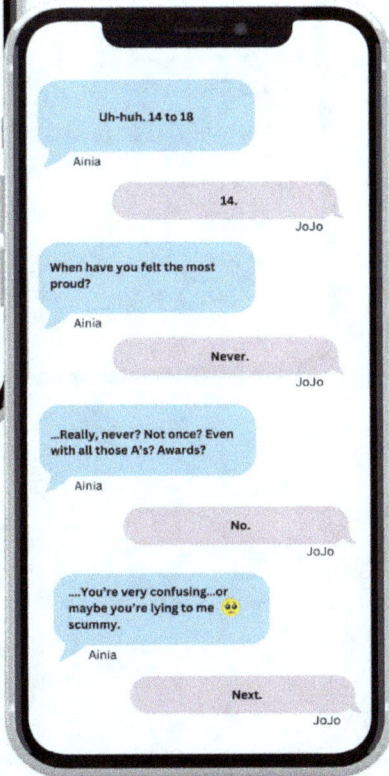

Uh-huh. 14 to 18

Ainia

14.

JoJo

When have you felt the most proud?

Ainia

Never.

JoJo

...Really, never? Not once? Even with all those A's? Awards?

Ainia

No.

JoJo

....You're very confusing...or maybe you're lying to me 🥺 scummy.

Ainia

Next.

JoJo

15 to 18

Ainia

15.

JoJo

Why're you all of a sudden cooperating????

Ainia

?

JoJo

You're going in order now even when I asked, oh so nicely before.

Ainia

We should reevaluate 'nicely'

JoJo

🙁

Ainia

Question.

JoJo

If you could change one thing about yourself, what would it be?

Ainia

Tricky. So many things.

JoJo

Like what?

Ainia

Not telling.

JoJo

Can't you be specific and not be so vague?????

Ainia

I don't have time.

JoJo

Yada Yada. (...)

Ainia

Ainia is typing...

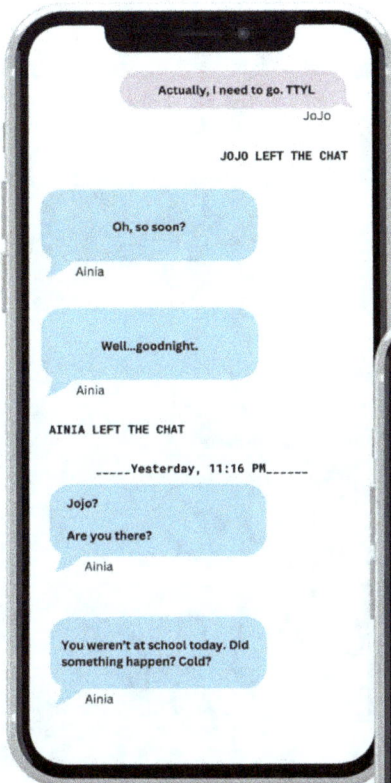

Actually, I need to go. TTYL

JoJo

JOJO LEFT THE CHAT

Oh, so soon?

Ainia

Well...goodnight.

Ainia

AINIA LEFT THE CHAT

_____Yesterday, 11:16 PM_____

Jojo?

Are you there?

Ainia

You weren't at school today. Did something happen? Cold?

Ainia

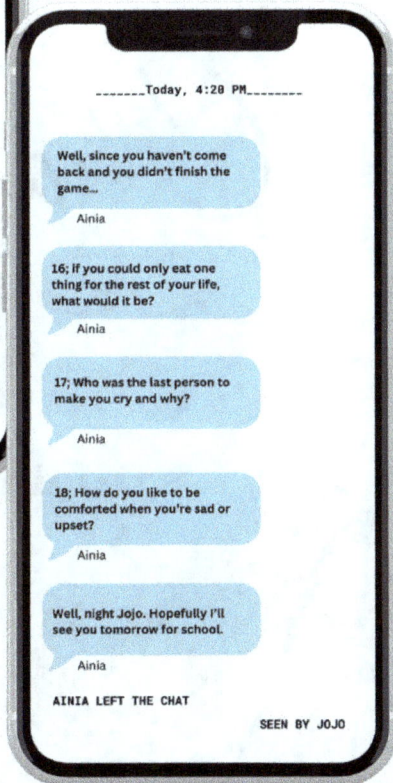

_____Today, 4:28 PM_____

Well, since you haven't come back and you didn't finish the game...

Ainia

16; If you could only eat one thing for the rest of your life, what would it be?

Ainia

17; Who was the last person to make you cry and why?

Ainia

18; How do you like to be comforted when you're sad or upset?

Ainia

Well, night Jojo. Hopefully I'll see you tomorrow for school.

Ainia

AINIA LEFT THE CHAT

SEEN BY JOJO

39

Chaotic Prose

Original Poetry

Love

By Mikayla Lewis

Love
Such a powerful word, yet only some know the meaning.

Is love a feeling?
Is love an action?
Is love good?
Is love bad?

For me, love is
looking at someone and feeling at home,
oversharing every bit of your day with that person so it
feels like they were there with you being vulnerable around
them and not caring about the potential backfires, and
loving everything about them.

Love is what you make it,
and when you find it, make the best out of it
and try to make it last
because you may not find it again.
Love

My Broken Household

By Mikayla Lewis

My household been broke since I was born.
It started with my moms drinking and smoking.
Continued with my dad never being in the picture,
and every time he was, something bad followed.

And if I don't get out now, it'll end with my life.
Or one of my brothers.
Or my sisters.
Or my moms.
And I can't let that happen.

The weight of this family falls on me, a 14-year-old.
But that's probably because
I put everyone else before me.

I always smile even when I'm not happy, and I give more
than I have to see others happy.
I'm broken, but I gotta get fixed.
I don't want my child to suffer this pain.

I'm broken because I sense that
I can't fix anything around me.
I'm broken because that's where I come from.
I'm broken because I allowed people to break me.
I'm broken.

Fighting Spirit by Safiya Gaskins

Regret

By Kamarie Jones

You're going to regret the day you lose her.

The times she begged you to love her
and she cried for your attention.

You know and see how beautiful she is,
but you don't appreciate her.

You look at her as if she's a random whore.
You make her question her self-worth.

She looks in the mirror, having doubts,
comparing herself to the people you like on Instagram.

She wishes she was one of them,
not knowing she was better.

She doesn't find the beauty within herself anymore.

She feels ugly.

You're going to regret the way you treated her.

I'm sorry she ever met you.

Why can't you love her the way she loves you?

You're Back

By Makayla Howard

You're back.
The thing that holds me back during opportunities.

The thing that makes me panic in the inside.

The thing that makes me so overwhelmed
with my thoughts.

You're back.

I can never get rid of you.

You are a part of me.

No one can see the panic attacks you give me.

No one can see how you shut down my body.

No one can see the pitch-black hole
in my heart because of you.

That piece missing is happiness.

Darkskin Girl

By Makayla Howard

Dark skin. The most hated skin color,
Yet the most beautiful.

Look at the *dark skin* girl over there,
Nature covering her skin.
Beauty shining throughout her skin.

Have you ever heard of the feminine urge?
She has the feminine urge
to connect with her ancestors,
To get in touch with her femininity
by wearing long skirts.
To walk barefoot.
To listen to Erykah Badu and Lauryn Hill.
To break generational curses.
To expand her knowledge.
To empower other women.
And most of all, to be soft.

Soul

By Kamarie Jones

I remember us first meeting.
The missing void in my heart was being filled.

My tears turned into happiness
and my sadness turned into smiles.

It was like my heart was being healed
until I realized love isn't supposed to make you feel
pain or a constant heartache.

Love is supposed to build you,
not slowly kill your soul.
Love is supposed be genuine,
and something that makes you happy.

If I knew your love would have made me hurt,
I would've never loved you.

You

By Kamarie Jones

I always told you how much I love you,
but to put it into the right words would be impossible.

My love for you feels forever lasting,
and you're the piece of my heart I needed.

You're my home. The home that's filled with flowers and
plays peaceful music.

With you, my heart dances
and never seems to break or ache.

You're my addiction that makes me feel
as if you're a drug;

you're a psychedelic and I'm just high.

I'm addicted to you.

I love you. <3 - k

~*Forbidden Love*~

By Nevaeh Fleming

You're so precious,
But this love is poison.

Why is this so addicting?

"Please don't leave," I plead.

I will still try to make you stay.

I want this to work.

Why are they in our business?
Go away! You make me sick!

Please stay. I won't be able to live.

I think you're pretty.

You say that I'm ugly.

You apologize.
I know you didn't mean it.

You're mad because you kept hearing
all the ignorant voices of others.

When will we be able to say those three words
and be able to mean it?

Why do I have to question you?
When will you stop second-guessing being with me?

We have everything when we're together.
Is this the reason they say we must be apart?
Are we too much for them?
Can they not comprehend this feeling?

Will they continue to bash us for falling in—
I will continue to cry for falling in—
You will continue to be mad for falling in—
We will keep falling in—

Deep
Deep
Mad
Forbidden love

Many Truths; One Lie

By Makayla Howard

Everybody's heard of Black Boy Joy
Or Black Girl Magic,
But have you ever seen it with your own eyes?

Like that girl who sits in the front of the classroom,
Always laughing and smiling,
Who believes she can be anything
She wants to be in life.

Her inspiration is through music.
She never misses a beat through her feet.
She isn't bothered by anything or what anyone says.

And most of all, she's a Black girl.

Unapologetically Black

By Nevaeh Fleming

We have lived a painful history.
Are the right and wrong things so hard to see?

People are in pain, and we do nothing.
This is robbery.

Resentful over and over because they aren't free.
They steal happiness and look the other way rudely.

People can't seem to come together and agree.
People try to protest, but it ends badly.
They stand for what they believe in, hoping to be free.
The government has failed;
the people abuse of authority.

You can choose who you want to be.
I'm an African descendant.
We are elegant, not messy.
I'm proud to be mixed.

I can guarantee
My peoples' clothes are unique and classy.
I have a really big and special family tree.
My peoples' music is beautiful and catchy.

Everyone is different, so why do they still disagree?
It's sad how some people don't accept others.
Everyone bleeds, everyone cries.
What don't you see?
Reality is harsh. People get treated unfairly.
For equality, you shouldn't have to pay a fee.

People still judge others. It's silly.
They speak up and still aren't heard. That pains me.
People shouldn't have to fight to be happy.

This poem is about my thoughts on gender equality and people being treated differently because of how they want to express themselves. It also has parts of my identity in the poem that express my love for being a proud African-American, and how I'm mixed. I appreciate my culture and I'm not ashamed of it. I am really proud to be Black because we are successful and beautiful.
I am unapologetically Black.

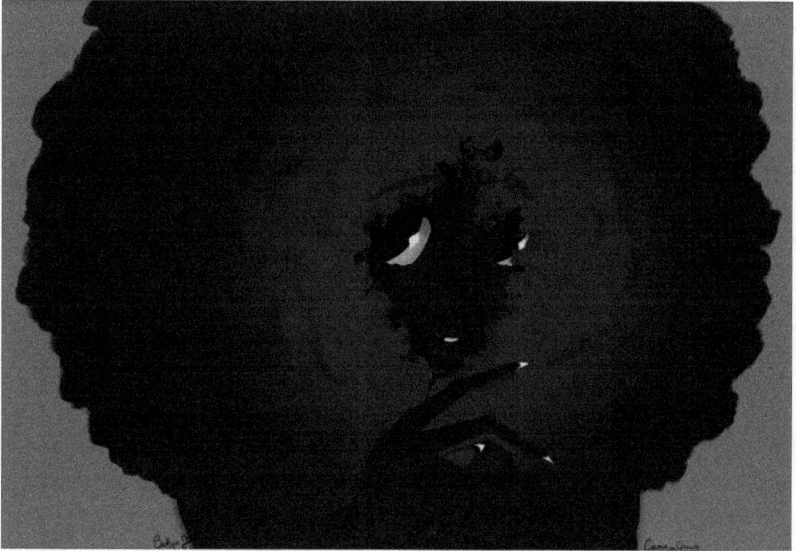

Cherry Red by Safiya Gaskins

Frozen

By Nevaeh Fleming

Iced over like December.
My name, I can't remember.

My head spinning,
Air is chilling,
Mood is killing,
Then my eyes are closing.

I'm shutting down.
Please, give me a blanket.

Time is running out.
First my feet, to legs, to mouth.
I'm freezing over from the inside out.

Loneliest girl is what they said.
Coldest girl is what I am.
Clocking out not a 9-5.

Don't come knocking.
I'm out.
I'm frozen.

What is love?

By Kamarie Jones

Is love what I feel around me?
Or is it the unknown feeling of happiness that I crave?

I feel loved. I think.

Is love supposed to make you cry
and make you feel the most unbearable pain?

Why does love hurt?

I never understood why feeling love make my heart ache
or makes me feel pain.

If this is love, then I don't want it.
I'd rather be alone and feel unloved.

I hate love. - k

Cold ways, Cold days

By Nevaeh Fleming

Cold can be quiet

Cold can leave you hurt

Cold can be matched

Cold can be ongoing

Cold will leave you shaking

Cold will make the heartbreak

Cold can make you cold

Cold can be inside and out

Bitter cold,

Sweet cold.

Humans can be cold

Me cold

We cold

He and she cold

Eat cold

Sleep cold

To be cold or not to be cold

By Steven Fairfax

Loveliest

By Nevaeh Fleming

She/he who makes me smile,
Gives me butterflies.

Oh, wow, their eyes!
Only they made my heart hurt.

Them, who's is the loveliest?
You, who tackles my soul.

That thing you do when you—
And that sound you make when you—
Don't let me forget when you—smile.

I could go on and on and on.
I'd scream it to the world,
I'd make them all jealous.

You, my treasure:
The loveliest you.

Below Zero

By Nevaeh Fleming

Dear ice princess,
Who watches her kingdom from afar,
Worried to spread her temperature around.

Caring for her kingdom,
Staying in her room.
Tea in the afternoon.

Same routine,
Same cuisine,
Her small view.

Who knew?
It's true,
She's cold.

Not mean,
Not sneaky,
Not rude.

She's freezing,
All alone
In her room,
Viewing the kingdom,
Caring for her people,
Loving her view,
Living with her condition.
Ice princess.

Rebirth

By Kamarie Jones

After this life I would like to be at peace
At a place where my soul and inner self can finally rest.

If I come back to earth, I'd hope to live as a peaceful
animal who's happy and has no worries.

Or maybe I can be where this being God is.

The thought of God existing brings me fear,
and yet comfort.

What if I've sinned too much to be forgiven,
and can never be at peace?

What if I never be at peace
and forever deal with my own ongoing hell?

I hope to be at peace
one day. - k

Confusion

By Nevaeh Fleming

To know,
To think.
Comprehending by guessing.

Learning, but seeing.
Seeing is believing.
Not believing, 'cause everything is lies.

Trying and failing,
Disappointment of so many,
Madness is swelling.

Lungs hurt from yelling,
Heartbroken from believing.
Hands shaking in the cold.

Eyes see blurs.
Tears are confirmed.
Blurred and confused.

Mess,
Mess,
Mess!

By Adrianna Pittman

Deep

By Nevaeh Fleming

I'm in deep.

No secrets,

No lies.

All truth, straight forward

Conversation about whatever.

Diving so deep,

It's almost scary.

I take a moment,

Almost questioning the depth,

But it continues

Sinking low,

Low and lower.

Sink to my heart

All from the very start.

Je te laisserai des mots

By Nevaeh Fleming

I leave you notes
Filled with characters
Describing my feelings for you.
I'm sorry I left you.
Day by day
I fade, but write to you.

I wait to write my next note
To you, of whom I can't get enough.
I am so attached to you.

I leave you notes.
Please realize
It was only you, my dear.

On again
inspired by Lauryn Hill

By Nevaeh Fleming

Nothing even matters at all.

The planet will continue to turn every day
Until the day it doesn't
Because life will end.
Not to be sad or depressed,
But nothing even matters at all.

Make mistakes.
Laugh, love, learn every day.
Days are days,
Good or bad,
'Cause nothing even matters at all!

Whether you make a change,
Or move at a slow pace,
Just remember: you will get up another day.
You're you; do life your own way
'Cause nothing even matters at all.

Happiness

By Kamarie Jones

I'm afraid of being happy.

Not because I'm afraid of it ending,
because eventually everything comes to an end.

Even life.

But…

the truth is, I'm afraid of being happy because the only
emotion that has ever made me feel something
is my own sadness.

What happens after I become happy?

Will I actually feel something?
or will I become completely numb? - *k*

Art Recently

By Nevaeh Fleming

I've been thinking about creative time.
Peace of mind,
Need to find
Something true, real and kind.

Light up my life.
You make me feel
My hard work, the most divine.

From fun to seriously,
Art works so mysteriously.

As I paint the sea,
My soul stares back at me.
The wave of love crashing
Into me,
I make art recently.

It Is a Crime

By Nevaeh Fleming

To enter the world
And grow up in this life
As the being you are,
So different, so you.

Is it a crime to be any less divine,
To not impress the people?
Your quiet nature,
Your fairy world you made,
Is being attacked.

Protect yourself.
It's not a crime to be any less divine
In this world or the next.
It's not a crime to be a fairy.
It's not a crime to be different.

April 22, 2022

By Nevaeh Fleming

On this day,
Feelings at bay,
They don't violently sway.
They stay.

Here in my heart
and processing always,
Like shopping with my cart,
Picking what to display always.

Someone steals my feelings away,
Racing and repeating like relay.
Why is this the price I pay?
Well, next month will be May.

Fresh start,
Or depressing depart?
Feelings separate and part ways
Like a flying dart.

Tomorrow is April 23, 2022.

To the Ones Who Hear

By Nevaeh Fleming

Tiny people, have you seen it all?
In the wall
You sit, you stall.
As I stand tall,
I fight the fall,
Trying not to let go of it all.

Answer the call.
Don't go to the mall.
As you sit and stall,
Await the fall.

Provide accusation
Your backup plan
As the tiny people listen in.
Stories began
As I ran
Toward the tiny people.

They see the tears.
The fight for self.
The fight of a person
Learning how to swim
As you drown.
Live.
And to the ones who hear,
Live!

Apartment Door

By Nevaeh Fleming

I watched you take out your key
to lock the door of your apartment.
I could tell you had been crying.
Sorry about your brother.
RIP.
This time, I thought you would come back.
Back to your apartment.
Back to your kids.
Back to your mother.
But you never did.

All your mother did was send help.
They came to check on your "welfare".
Instead of sending help, they sent six rounds.
Warning shots to you.
You, the innocent.
You the distraught older brother
Mourning your brother's death.

To that cop, he only saw a threat,
Unworthy of the gun he had.
Possessing a weapon meant for protection,
Only to deliver injustice to you.
Your keys dropped,
For you had been shot.
AR-15 rifle straight to your back.
All he got was eighty hours without pay,
Then he continued to work away.

Now, your mother and kids watch as you lay flat.
Your mother is reminded of you every time

Another cop steals a young Black life.
You were only twenty-five.
Your kids needed you alive.

No justice, no peace!
Say his name:
AARON CAMPBELL

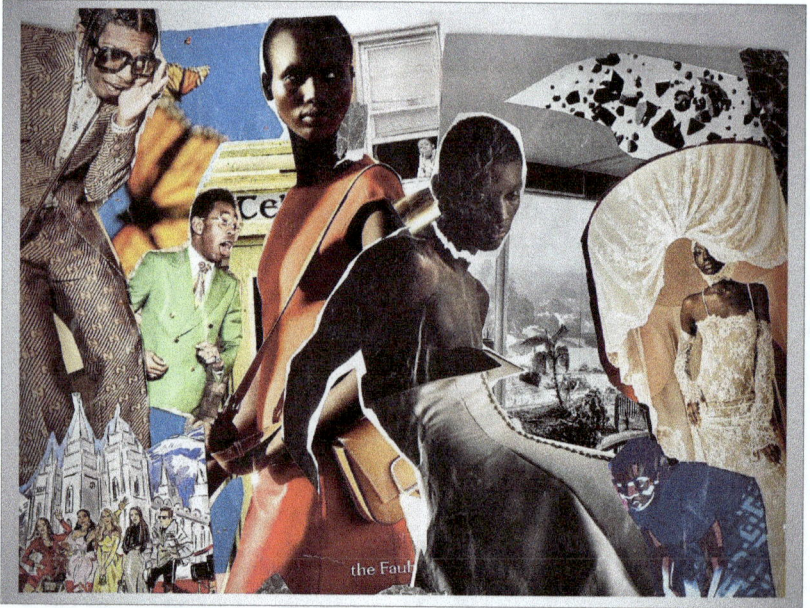

By Safiya Gaskins

Language In Which We Say

By Nevaeh Fleming

Language In Which You Say PT 1

The connection of words.
The minds that think same letters,
Same words, but different view.
The meaning is all up to you.

Starting from drawing,
Writing is a form of art.
Symbols that move mountains.
Words that start wars.
Worlds together brought to you by words.
Language: something you don't have to say out loud.

Some form words because the feeling
Of being able to have that word.
The strength to speak,
To speak in language or languages,
To say the thoughts you have.
The thoughts that may or may not be words
Feel so complex, no language could say.

To bury words or want to say
You have a language,
You say 'cause you feel or not feel.
You say, you simply say.
You think in language,
The world and language,
The many beautiful languages
In which you say.

Language In Which You Say PT 2

You act because you thought
The motion of a language,
The physical state of words
To do what you think,
To act because you wished
To move at your mercy.

Words that leave you motionless,
Words that caused
The act because of that word.
The movement created,
All starting from,
All circling back to
Everything centered by language.

Language In Which We Say PT 3

What is your language?
How do you choose to communicate?
Even if you didn't choose
The default language, do you speak?
How does your language speak to you?
You and yours?

Fight or compromise.
Battle and makeup.
Internal, external and all in between,
Willing, by default.

Sekai Heiwa
(World Peace)

By Nevaeh Fleming

Imagine the unlimited possibilities you're granted
When you're at peace.
Now, our minds are free to roam anywhere.
Pressure to do this and that is vanquished.
Everything we want can be achieved through hard work.
Love is sweeter than ever before.
It's time to be aware of everyone, Sonder.

We left the fighting behind
For peace.
We left the wars behind
For peace.
NO killings because weapons are banned.
NO bad people
Because they have been treated with proper care.
We reflect on the past and vow it will never happen again.
The lives lost will never be forgotten.
It's our unseen duty to remember, so don't forget.

We know this path is the hardest one to take.
Even so, we have never regretted wanting it.
This world makes me experience Hiraeth.
It's so beautiful.
So green.
So prosperous.
Everywhere you look is filled with iridescent beauty.
No one could have known this is what happens
When we are at peace.

It's about time we change our ways.
Everything eco-friendly.
Clean air.
Clean streets.
Clean people.
We have converted plenty
To be at peace with our surroundings.
We must protect this ethereal planet.

We prepare this world for our children,
For their children, and the children after them.
We polish this emerald jewel accordingly.
We prepare the truth for our new leaves,
Educating them, watching them grow.
These new leaves are the most important of all.
With all the education provided, new ideas will form
and we will continue on.

As these new leaves develop, some will be opposed.
This is all right. We know no one and nothing is perfect.
Peace won't come because you wish for it.
Peace is a process, but knowing this
Has made the path a possible tangible thing.

Cheers to peace and love.
Cheers to dreams and hard work.
Cheers to the new world,
Our journey to Sekai Heiwa.

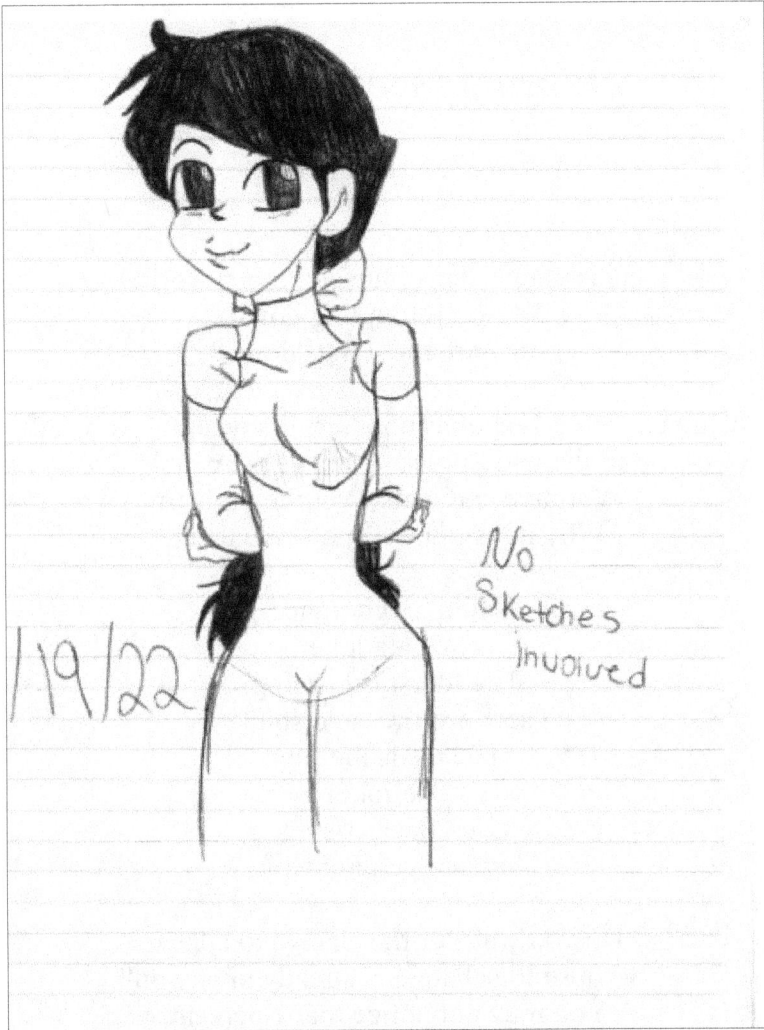

By Adrianna Pittman

What do we wait for??

By Nevaeh Fleming

This planet. This blue and green world.
Why is it trending down?
Why are the trends down?

Climate change is not as popular. It's dead. It drowned.
In the widespread ocean of the people
Who live and walk over the problem,
Why not sit down and solve them?

Human ignorance.
What a joke!
The forest is burning.
There are fires and smoke.
The ice is melting.
No joke!
Sea levels rising.
How are you not woke?

Do you wait for the change to appear
Because the change is already upon you?
You may not notice that 1 percent,
But the planet makes it decent.

Come together to save the world
One step at a time.
Hopefully, we will make it in time.
Because what do we wait for??

Untitled Poem

By Rahkeam Pickens

The sun seldom shines.
You break free of the constraints,
sprouting from your planter.

You can grow and go anywhere they say,
but always picking the weeds around you—
they leave you behind.

Brighter than the sun, taller than the empire.
You're the brightest dandelion in the valley.
The gently sloping hills became
Rugged and rough ledges.

The youth that skipped in the blankets of grass
Gave way to lorries and billowing smokestacks.
You're one in a million, uniquely you.
All that remains are dreams of yesterday.
Rebuild with what remains,
Brighter than the sun, taller than the empire.

Addiction

By Kamarie Jones

I knew I was obsessed when your love felt like a drug.
It started to become more of a need than a want.

I craved you and needed you
as if you were my personal dose.

I couldn't stop craving you and became *addicted*,
but your love was a toxic addiction.

Never again.

:(

I hate the fact that you've become my poison,
and it's weakening my mind.

Your words are starting to feel like kryptonite
and I'm superman with only one weakness,
and it's *you. - k*

Troubles

By Nevaeh Fleming

I wish I could throw away all my troubles.
Maybe stuff them all in a bubble.
Trouble kills the mood.
Troubles, like no food.
Don't let me start.
Troubles stab my heart.

Speaking of troubles, I'm always so mad.
It's little things that can make me sad.
Work brings trouble.
Outside brings trouble.
Inside brings trouble.
Where is *my* bubble?

Index

About TMA

Thurgood Marshall Academy is a law-themed public charter high school in Washington, D.C.'s Ward 8. It was founded on U.S. Supreme Court Justice Thurgood Marshall's belief that all children have the right to a first-class education.

The school opened in 2001 with 80 ninth-graders, and added a grade each year. By 2021, TMA served 367 students in grades 9-12.

Thurgood Marshall Academy's mission is to prepare students to succeed in college and actively engage in our democratic society. As the first and only law-related charter school in Washington, D.C., the school's goal is to help students develop their own voice by teaching them the skills lawyers have—the ability to solve complex problems, think critically, and advocate persuasively for themselves and their communities.

To accomplish its mission, TMA functions as both a school and youth development organization by integrating a rigorous college-preparatory curriculum with in-school and after-school support programming, such as academic tutoring, enrichment activities, a Summer Prep program for rising 9th graders, and one-on-one college guidance. To provide these supplemental programs, Thurgood Marshall Academy has developed a network of over 65 partnering organizations that provide financial and in-kind support and connect the school with over 300 volunteers.

About The Contributors

TJ Hendrix

I am a veteran teacher from Little Rock, Arkansas, and I have been involved in student arts projects such as this one since I was younger than many of these students. I am now going into my second year as an English Language Arts teacher at TMA, and it truly feels like a home for me. These student artists are phenomenal, and I could not be prouder of their dedication. Providing outlets for student voices, whether through poetry, stories, drawings, or collages, is important to the development of confidence and awareness for all students. Though this is not the first anthology produced by TMA, it is the first in a while. We are quite proud of the work the students did and we hope that you enjoyed this book.

Steven Fairfax

I am a junior at Thurgood Marshall Academy. I am a passionate student who enjoys music, basketball, and drawing.

Nevaeh Fleming

My name is Nevaeh Shiane-Marie Fleming. I am 18 as of the Nov. 13, 2022. I'm a senior who started attending TMA in 2019, and I will graduate in 2023. I'm very interested in creative writing and reading fiction. I also love poetry and listening to spoken word poetry. I'm a starter on our school's volleyball team and love to play softball. The reason I write is to share my opinions, which have been shaped by the famous poets whose work I enjoy.

Safiya Gaskin

Hello, my name is Safiya Gaskin, and I am the artist behind some of the pieces in this year's anthology. I am 16 years old, and I've been a student at TMA for almost two years now. I am a part of this wonderful anthology project that you are reading. I am also part of several extracurricular programs, but my main interests are creating art and fashion design. I create my art mostly for my happiness, but I really enjoy it when others like the way I express myself. This joy makes it fun to create for others as well. I like to give people a glimpse into my mind to see the thoughts in my head. I want people to see my creative vision. That is one of the main reasons I create art.

Makayla Howard

My name is Makayla Howard. I am 16 years old, and I've been attending TMA for three years now. I am officially an 11th grader and I've been writing poems since 10th grade. I write poetry to express how I'm feeling at that moment. Most of the time, I am inspired by music, especially J. Cole. I'm really excited for people to finally see my work!

Kamarie Jones

My name is Kamarie Jones and I'm 17 years old. I've been attending Thurgood Marshall since 9th grade, the year of 2019. My interests include reading, writing poetry, rowing, baking and cooking. At school, I participate in the TMA Anthology Project and Book Club. I write because writing to me is a form of self-expression, and an art that allows me to feel at peace. I prefer to write because it is a way for me to cope with different emotions :)

Mikayla Lewis

Mikayla Lewis was a ninth-grade student at Thurgood Marshall Academy during the 2021 - 2022 school year. She is a gifted poet and performer. Though she is no longer a student at TMA, she will always be a Warrior!

Rahkeam Pickens

I am Rahkeam Pickens. I am 17, and have been a student at TMA since ninth grade in 2019. Currently, I am a member of the TMA Newspaper Club and the TMA Anthology Project. I am interested in politics, history, and, oddly enough, sociology. Outside of TMA, I am a fellow in Seeding Disruption REMIX, here in D.C. I choose to write because it is an outlet that no one can take from you once it's gifted. Put your thoughts in pen and you can't be matched.

Adrianna Pittman

My name is Adrianna Noelle Pittman. I am a 17-year-old attending Thurgood Marshall. My time here began back in 2019, and now I am a senior, set to graduate in 2023. I enjoy drawing, writing, and reading fan fiction. I love writing scripts and outlines for future subjects. I like to draw to make a compelling story that my selected audience and I will enjoy. I've joined numerous clubs that I enjoy greatly like DND, art, anime, books, newspapers, and anthology. The reason I write/type stories is because I enjoy it. It's a good way to pass the time, and in the future, I'd like to put them to better use when I hopefully learn to code. I draw because I want to; I've been drawing for years, and have been growing. Even now, I am still improving.

Henry Walker

Hello, reader. My name is Henry Walker. I am 17 years old and have been a TMA student for 3.2 years. The anthology program has been the only one I have been interested in since I joined TMA back in 2019. I have hobbies such as exercising and sports, but I don't do much outside school, but work. I write because I have this insatiable desire to help the world. I feel I should start somewhere, and writing just fell into my lap. It has helped me express myself, and the future is bright from my perspective. Thank you all for listening. Enjoy the rest of your evening.